Until Heaven Then My Friend

Life's Journey For Your Beloved Dog

Tana Osborn

Tana Osborn

Published in Powell Butte, Oregon by Updraft Publishing

Library of Congress Data Available Upon Request.
ISBN-10: 0991472616
ISBN-13: 978-0-9914726-1-1

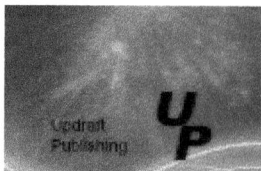

Have you ever shed tears at the earthly death of a beloved dog?

Ever wondered if you'd be with your furry friend
or friends again?

Dared to look in the scriptures to find
anything at all that might tell you that
your beloved dog's journey ends safely in heaven?

The reassurance you are looking for is found in God's word
and is brought out in this book.
Even though the Bible is meant to lay out
the plan for human redemption,
there are countless scriptures that clearly and directly provide
a peace that will flood your soul, giving you peace and comfort.

Dedication

In honor of one of my very best friends, Angus, who through his death encouraged me to write this book to reassure myself, but also encourage others that we will be with our beloved dog friends forever in heaven.

"ANGUS"

UNTIL HEAVEN THEN
MY FRIEND
WHEN I SEE YOU AGAIN

Contents

Introduction   Pg 7
Chapter 1 A Binding Friendship   Pg 19
Chapter 2 How Do You Get To Heaven?   Pg 27

PART 1 WHY WOULDN'T THERE BE ANIMALS IN
HEAVEN?

Chapter 3 His Creation   Pg 35
Chapter 4 Animals Are Important To God   Pg 37
Chapter 5 Animals Are A Shoe-In   Pg 43
Chapter 6 Body, Soul & Spirit   Pg 47
Chapter 7 How Our Spirit Differs From Animals   Pg 57

PART 2 WAITING FOR YOU IN HEAVEN

Chapter 8 God Knows You & Loves You   Pg 63
Chapter 9 God Loves To Give Us Good Gifts   Pg 67
Chapter 10 Your In Charge   Pg 71
Chapter 11 Your Dog Is Covered   Pg 73
Chapter 12 What We Know Of Heaven   Pg 75

PART 3 INTERESTING POSSIBILITIES!
(What Do You Think?)

Chapter 13 Conversation For The Birds   Pg 81
Chapter 14 Talking "Human"   Pg 83
Chapter 15 What Does The Lord Tell You?   Pg 87

Notes   Pg 89

Collies of every color. Each with their unique spirit. One, in particular, started me on the journey of discovering just how special a dog could become in the human life.

Introduction

Have you ever seriously pondered whether you would ever be with your beloved dogs for eternity? Maybe you just hope that you will. Maybe you have resigned yourself to never seeing them again. What if you had overwhelming reassurance that those dogs or pets that you so treasured on earth were in heaven waiting for you? Would that give you hope? Would it ease the grief you feel over losing them?

I wrote this book because I needed to know without a shadow of a doubt that I would be with my beloved doggie friends again and forever in heaven. I hadn't really given it much thought until a few years ago. Maybe because I am getting older (and wiser), thinking of heaven more or maybe because of the powerful connections I have made with my furry friends in recent years. Whatever the reason, I felt strongly that this book was needed to help bring peace to the many people who can't imagine heaven without their beloved dog friends.

There are many well known theologians, authors and speakers who do believe that animals and thus, our pets, go to heaven, but I wanted the "evidence" to be so clearly found that it wouldn't take a theologian to find it. So, I'd like to point out that I do not hold any theological degrees, yet God's word offers us an abundance of reassurance that the average layperson can find when looking. I believe that is one of the greatest sources of comfort to those of us who love our dogs so dearly. The answer is there for us all.

The first couple chapters of this book speak of how important our dogs are to us and how we can know we will be in heaven together when it's our turn to go. If you are actively grieving and just want to start embracing the reassurance you need that your friend is safe in heaven, then feel free to begin with chapter 3. Through this book, for me, the issue is settled in my heart. I hope when you are done with this book, it will be for you too. And that you can say confidently, "until heaven then, my friend, when I see you again."

A Couple Of My Cherished Friends

I have lost two dogs in recent years that I was strongly bonded with. Time does help, but it is still so hard to lose those we love, even our cherished dogs. In my upcoming book, Celebrate Your Pet - Turning Grief Into Sweet Memories, I share some ideas on how to enjoy the wonderful memories you have while you wait for your turn to join them in heaven.

It is a strange, but awesome feeling to bond intimately with a dog. It is like your spirits are woven together in your soul and theirs. You are not just a part of each others life, but you are a part of each other. It is a connection that many non-dog owners don't understand and even dog owners can miss sometimes. It is about a relationship with your dog, even a "friendship." Relationships with people can differ for a variety of reasons. So it is with our dogs. The strength of a friendship forged takes commitment, compassion and work, whether human to human or human to dog.

Oh dear, what delusions of grandeur to think we could hold down our current jobs at the time, raise 2 kids, plus train all these dogs for such an undertaking. Needless to say, we ended up with 4 pets.

My beloved friend, Sage, was a blue merle collie. She was the sweetest, most loyal companion I had ever had. We had 3 other collies at the time, but Sage and I quickly connected. Yes, we had 4 collies, one of each color, in order to do a dog ministry. They all were good dogs, but the bond with Sage was something I had never experienced before. It was like the essence of who we were being intertwined.

When Sage was still a puppy, both her third eyelids, located below her eyes, grew up over her eye, sort of like a tumor. It grew to the point of covering a good portion of her eyes. Her eyes were irritated and draining all the time.

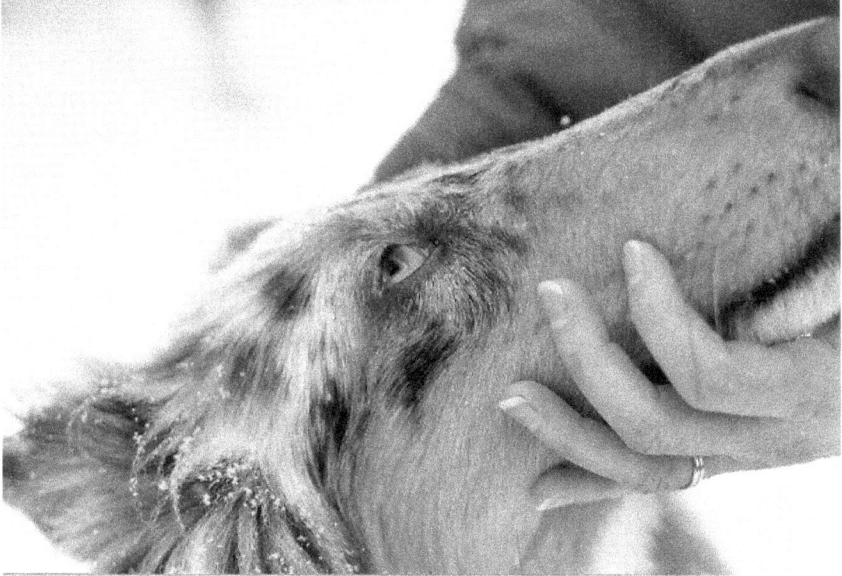

Her retinas were detaching as well. Her vision was limited. It amazes me how dogs can be so resilient and adapting though.

We took Sage to an eye specialist. After all non-invasive treatments were tried, she surgically removed the part of the eyelids that were covering her eyes. We were told that it would likely grow back and it did. We kept it at bay with nutrition, eye drops and natural therapies. I learned to see for her, telling her when to step up or helping her avoid running into the other dogs. She learned to trust me. I believe she felt the love I had for her deep in her soul. I had some rough times myself when we were together. She always seemed to know. She would come sit or lay down beside me.

Sage had to have her paw on me whenever she was next to me. I suppose many people could give different reasons for this. I think the most obvious is that due to her lack of vision, it gave her a sense of comfort. Looking back at it though, understanding more intricately the bond we shared, I wonder if it was partly that she was trying to give me comfort.

We were both tough though, yet gentle spirited and we just seemed to understand each other. I truly felt that she was my very best friend. Even though we couldn't articulate in each other's native language, we understood each other deep in our spirit.

When she was 9 years old, I knew something was wrong with her even before she gave me any obvious reason to suspect anything. She just didn't seem as happy. She seemed to be struggling, but I wasn't sure why. Sage was always a strong dog, very tolerant of whatever needed to be done with her. It was difficult to tell sometimes when she wasn't feeling well because she would rarely whine or whimper. She just always tried to comply with whatever was asked of her. Even when she almost broke her leg from running into the porch when she was a puppy, she didn't whine. She definitely demonstrated a high tolerance for pain.

Shortly after her 9th birthday, she began licking her leg to the point of producing big blister looking sores. When we went for a walk, she would take a few steps then lay down. I'd coax her to keep going, then she'd take a few steps and lay down again. It became evident that she was trying hard to comply, but she was experiencing pain with walking.

I took her to the veterinarian. After he examined her, he said the licking of her leg that was producing sores was her way of providing a distraction from the pain she was feeling elsewhere in her body.

Based on how she was holding and using her limbs, he felt she had an autoimmune disorder that was affecting her joints severely. He also said her eyes were not producing any lubrication at all, which was also a source of discomfort.

He told me that any therapies at this time would likely not help her much.

I feel strongly and the Bible tells us that God put humans in charge of the animals. We need to make decisions for them as we are moved in our heart to do. Sage was my very dear friend, my most loyal companion and had been for 9 years. I did not want her to leave me, but I felt so strongly I needed to let her go. I had already sensed that she was struggling even before the outward signs. Even though I knew she would hang tough for me the best she could, I felt that it would not serve any purpose for her to allow her to suffer. I knew it would only get worse for her. I decided to have her put down. That was one of the hardest, most heart wrenching moments of my entire life. It is one of the few times in my life that I truly sobbed uncontrollably.

Even though I know death from this earth is inevitable for us all, I still weakly question whether I did the right thing. My most loyal companion, the only living soul that truly understood me was gone. I missed her and still miss her.

After losing Sage, I didn't ever want a dog again. The pain in losing them was too great. After a few months went by, however, my teenage daughter came to me and said,

"Mom, I have been observing you and I think you need to get another dog." How funny, those were her exact words.

She had recently adopted a second dog, but because we were renting at the time, we could only have so many dogs. She found a home for that second dog so that I could get another dog. What a selfless act that I so appreciate to this day. After going back and forth about it and researching some different options, I decided I'd start looking.

Where I was working at the time, a colleague had been allowed to bring his Australian Shepherd to work every day. He and his wife bred them and had many of them at their home. I told him that I was thinking about a toy Australian Shepherd that I found listed on Craigslist. I had the person bring the dog to where I worked. I wanted my co-worker to meet the dog too. I was afraid of falling in love too quick and maybe making a poor choice.

The owner of the dog had said that the dog was friendly, but wouldn't come up to people. He said that he often would run in his crate frightened. When the dog came in the front door, he came up to me immediately. He started rubbing on my legs. I squatted down to greet him. He was the most affectionate little guy. Our hearts seemed to intertwine in seconds. I was in love in a matter of moments. I wanted him. When my colleague said, "if you don't buy him I will," I quickly gave the guy the money and told my colleague, "MINE!" In essence, GET AWAY! HE IS MINE!

Wow! What a sweet little guy. Being the nursing director at an assisted living community and because my colleague had been bringing his dog to work, I was allowed to do so. I felt tremendously blessed to be able to bring him with me every day.

We spent our breaks together playing Frisbee or ball. Sometimes we'd take a walk. Sometimes we would visit the residents. Although I was too busy to bring him out of the office a lot, I did do so when I could. Many of the assisted living residents loved to visit him or watch him do tricks.

One day, I had little Angus "say his prayers" for the resident who had her apartment across from my office. She was so tickled by that. I heard her tell people about it, over and over, for months afterward.

He brought joy to many of the residents, even just being in my office. They would pass by the window smiling and giggling as he would be sprawled out on the desk, sitting in the chair or laying down in the bookshelf.

Many of the residents loved dogs, but couldn't have any due to their physical or cognitive limitations, so having visits brought many of them a great deal of joy.

After seeing the joy and smiles that Angus brought, I decided I wanted to do a dog ministry, doing simple skits and tricks for assisted living residents around the area. I thought it might be nice to have another Australian Shepherd and start working toward that goal. That is when I got Boots and started Aussie Antics Ministry.

It was also about that time, I started working from home. Unfortunately, I was a bit strapped for cash as I attempted to get a business up and running. I didn't train the dogs as much as I had wanted. The stress of other things going on served enough of a distraction to keep the dog ministry at bay.

Angus and Boots though, bonded with each other strongly. He was so good to her. She looked to him for many things. He would protect her, clean her ears for her and was very tolerant of her puppy hood. We all had a great time together.

Then one day, we all went to the canal. Angus loved to fetch sticks or anything else you wanted to throw for him. He would get so excited to play fetch in the water. Like an obsessed excitement. He loved it! But that day, the fun quickly turned to sorrow.

He started showing symptoms when we got home from the canal. Things progressed quickly after that. We fervently drove him to the veterinarian. It was rush hour and our veterinarian was over 30 minutes a way in normal traffic. He was barely alive when we reached the doctor's office. His lungs were already full of blood and his heart was no longer working adequately. His blood pressure was so low, it was unobtainable. Due to that, they couldn't even start an IV for fluid replacement, which may or may not have bought time to repair the heart surgically... The veterinarian suspected it was chordae tendineae rupture. Small chords known as chordae tendineae connect the valve leaflets to the heart muscle. These tendineae connect the valve leaflets to the heart muscle. These chords prevent the leaflets of the valve from being forced open backwards during the powerful contraction of the heart. Apparently, it is not uncommon in toy breeds for these chordae tendineae to rupture, quickly causing heart failure and blood back up in the lungs. In the course of just over an hour, my friend was suddenly gone. He was a couple months shy of his 4th birthday.

Boots was 1 yr 10 months old at the time. She was noticeably sad and confused. For a while, she wouldn't even come up to me. That was so hard as I wanted her to know that I was there for her. I tried to spend extra time with her, which helped. Even then, it wasn't quite the same. She had looked to him frequently for her confidence. For months, she would go off by herself. She just didn't have the same zest. We both missed his vibrant energy.

Angus was a sprightly little guy. He seemed to enjoy life and anything we did. When he was chilling, you could usually find him at my feet or in my lap. He followed me from room to room. He was part of my everyday routine.

He even helped me in my online business, with photos, stories and videos. Once, I did a slide show of Angus helping me make a Herbalife nutrition shake. Then of course, let him have a sip.

I start every morning with a Herbalife shake. Every day, he would hear the blender going and get so excited. I started letting him lick the blender as I poured out my nutrition shake into my glass. It was part of our daily ritual. Then he would stare at me expectantly while I drank it, sometimes with a soft whimper. He was waiting for me to finish and go dry my hair.

Another habit we got into was I would kick the ball for him while I dried my hair. I sometimes tired of this ritual, but I did it because it made him so happy. Funny thing, but that was one of the things I missed the most when he was gone.

We were together all throughout the day, then he would often snuggle in the crick of my bent legs at night. I cannot adequately express how deeply painful it was to lose this little guy. It was nearly, literally unbearable. But then, somewhere in that grief, it was as if the Lord encouraged my spirit, reassuring me that Angus was okay. That he was in heaven with Him. And that he was with my other dog Sage. That he would be waiting for me and any other doggie friends that I may have on earth in the meantime.

In my spirit, I felt nudged to write this book, not only to further reassure myself, but to reassure the many others who struggle with whether their beloved pets will be with them in heaven. I learned that it is not goodbye forever, but "until heaven then my friend."

*****

By reading this book, I want you to comfortably get to the same place. You know that for many, the bond forged between master/owner and dog can be just as strong, if not stronger, than a human to human bond. Many non-dog owners don't understand this. You may even have been ridiculed for the grief you feel for your lost pet. Of course, we love our family members and human friends, but for many a dog fulfills deep emotional needs that aren't met with human to human relationships. And our dogs are part of our everyday routine.

When we connect deeply with our dog, we are joined together in spirit, our innermost self. (More on this later). This bonding may vary from pet to pet. At some level though, when you are responsible for taking care of a living soul, bonds are made.

He/she is there when you wake up, when you go to sleep, comforts you when you are sad or grumpy, forgives you when you don't take him for a walk, shares joy with just having you in their presence ...

When your dog is gone, it may be that many of your daily routines have changed. This is a big part of why grieving this loss can be even more difficult than say, a family member that you love dearly, but you only saw a couple times a year. A dog is part of your everyday life and this alone can make the grieving process a difficult one.

Those who have lost a beloved pet understand the point I am trying to make, but a little disclaimer here. I am simply talking about these pets that we have charge over becoming like part of the family. Obviously, if we had to take care of a human family member or an animal family member and for some reason we could only save or help one of them, our human family member would take priority, but you'd still make sure your furry friend was also taken care of. We can love both and each is a part of our life.

Just as human relationships have similarities and uniqueness, so does our relationships with our pets. Let's say Uncle Fred dies. He is family, but you haven't seen him for 40 years. You probably don't have strong emotional ties to Uncle Fred as he wasn't part of your everyday life. That loss will not be felt in the same way as if someone you have lived with for 40 years died. That is all I am saying.

It is important to note that even though grief generally fluctuates through several stages, everyone grieves in their unique way. There can be many personal variables at any given time in someone's life. Over the many years as a nurse, I witnessed grief in many forms. You need to allow yourself to grieve your loss and accept the fact that you don't have to grieve like someone else or worse yet, like they think you should. This is especially noteworthy when it comes to grieving the loss of a cherished pet. Even well meaning people may not understand why you are so sad over the loss of "just a dog,," but you know why. Many people will understand your sadness, but some won't. That's okay. Allow yourself to grieve and cherish the good memories of your friend.

One last thing, I would like to reiterate that I do not hold any theological degrees. It is the greatest hope I offer in this book as the "evidence" is clear to even a layperson, like myself. It is all right there in God's word.

You can add to that reassurance, the fact that well known theologians and scholars agree that animals, including our pets, will be in heaven. People such as Billy Graham, Jim Daly, Randy Alcorn, C.S. Lewis, Martin Luther, Peter Kreeft and over 50 others that were found just in my simple research alone. Not to mention eyewitness accounts of some people who had a glimpse of heaven, while being clinically dead and in the process of medical personnel bringing them "back" in resuscitation efforts.

So add to your reassurance that Bible scholars, literature, commentaries and interviews confirm the interpretation of God's holy scriptures, which clearly indicate that animals, including your pets, will be in heaven.

All the input is valuable to the contents of this book, but I want you to see that you don't have to go past picking up the Bible to gain the reassurance, that you will indeed be reunited with your beloved dog(s) in heaven. I encourage you to pray about some of these scriptures and let the Lord bring comfort and clarity to your spirit.

I sincerely hope that reading this book will solidify it for you as it did for me, so that you too can confidently say in your heart, "until heaven then my friend, when I see you again."

Chapter 1
A Binding Friendship

Grieving the loss of a beloved pet may not be understood by everyone. Some people are even ridiculed. Yet anyone who has had the privilege of sharing part of their life's journey with a beloved pet knows there is a binding friendship between human and animal. These deep relationships are usually with a dog, but it could be a cat, horse or other 4-legged furry friend. It could even be with a less traditional "pet." Maybe a hedgehog or a turtle. Neither with a whole lot of fur, but still a "friend."

Yet, there are many reasons the dog has earned the title, "man's best friend." Their unconditional love, commitment and loyalty to name a few. Yet, each human dog interaction has unique qualities depending on the relationship forged between the human spirit and their dog.

Our relationships with our dog friends can bond us like family. Certainly, dogs have earned their right many times over to be called "man's best friend" because of their loyalty, helpfulness and affection that they often provide. They bring us comfort, joy and even relaxation. And we can brighten their life by reciprocating that friendship.

Some dogs help people physically with their health and in practical ways, such as helping people with disabilities. There have been several well publicized studies that show dogs can help us by decreasing stress and anxiety in our lives. Physiological studies have demonstrated that dogs can actually lower our blood pressure and cause a boost in our immune system.

Now, I know that sometimes they misbehave and raise our blood pressure, but these times should be momentary. If not, a professional dog behaviorist might be called upon to help in assisting with better human dog communication. Each dog and human have their unique personality, so sometimes it is just a matter of finding that connection. Sometimes a good book on human dog relationships can help people strengthen this communication. And of course, consistent expectations.

Studies have also shown that dogs can pick up on the most subtle non-verbal communication, even more so than humans. They have an amazing ability to pick up on energy being released as well. They often act on that energy accordingly, whether good or bad. Many of us have certainly experienced concern when having a dog near someone who is fearful of dogs. Sometimes that negative energy can be seen as a threat or be misinterpreted, which occasionally can cause a dog to be aggressive.

Some dogs can even pick up on environmental clues that we, as humans, are totally unaware of. They have a sort of sixth sense or extrasensory perception that involves picking up information that isn't received through the regular physical senses, but rather they are sensed by the mind. This ability combined with their excellent sensory ability creates many dogs that are hyper-intuitive.

It could be you are going along happily on your walk and your dog all the sudden gets tense, looking back and forth, his gait changes and maybe he starts sniffing the air. He is trying to tell you that there is possible danger nearby, maybe human, maybe animal. Pay attention!

Dogs can also warn people when indoors. Sometimes an intruder intending harm may be many yards from your home causing your dog to become tense or hyper vigilant. Or maybe it is a storm that may be approaching and they start getting anxious. So, it is not just our energy that they are attuned to, but also their environment. It is incredible all the things dogs can do. Some can even literally save our life.

There are dogs that can tell a diabetic that their blood sugar is getting too high or too low, or that someone is about to have a seizure or some other catastrophic event. It is amazing! They can also be trained to help humans with activities of daily living, such as dressing, turning the light on or off or helping people with tasks related to vision or hearing, when someone is blind or deaf.

They can deliver messages for us as some did in battle, they can sniff out bombs or drugs or even physically protect us. They might even provide mouse control. Go terriers! The list goes on and on. Sometimes they don't do anything, but give us company as our loyal friend. This attribute by itself can bring us tremendous joy and sets them apart as "man's best friend."

The many things they teach us

Dogs can play many roles in our lives. They teach us the responsibility of caring for another living soul. (I will tackle that "soul" subject later on). And dogs can offer many analogies to our relationship with our Heavenly Father.

Below are a few things that our furry friends can teach us in life. I am sure these are not new things for anyone, but they are worth mentioning before we move on. I want to illustrate these qualities that the dog possesses because it reminds us that they have spirits too, each unique and special to God.

Thinking about how and why these little friends impact our lives is really critical to understanding why it is not likely that losing them from our earthly home is forever. I believe God's word gives us much reassurance that we will be reunited.

1. **Unconditional Love**: No animal (or often human) offers unconditional love like a dog. I am sure there are exceptions to this, but this is the most common reason that the dog got nicknamed, "man's best friend." This is a huge reason why people love dogs. It is also why it is so heartbreaking when people mistreat their dog because a dog offers so much and really doesn't expect a lot in return.

We live in a society where so many people, young and old, don't understand what unconditional love really means. A dog can teach us a lot about this, which can improve our bond with our dog, but also ripple out to our human relationships. Most importantly our relationship with our Savior.

With our dog friends, it doesn't matter whether we have mustard all over our face, whether we walk funny or are less than perfect. (This is a good thing as we are all less than perfect). A beloved dog loves us just for us. We are the most important thing in their world. We can be boring, grumpy or sleepy. We can be hyper, talkative or quiet. We might be the sharpest tool in the shed or the dullest. It just doesn't matter to our dog. They just want to be with us. Of course, they love doing fun stuff with us too, but they typically will follow our lead and just be happy sharing whatever activity we want to do, whether it is playing ball or taking a nap. Being careful to match up the breed with our personality and energy level can improve this bonding of spirits and happiness for both.

Jesus loves us this way. He loves us just for us, on good days and not so good days. We don't have to be perfect. Even when we mess up, He still loves us. He'll spend time with us anytime we want to spend time with Him, whether we are boring, quiet or noisy. And yes, He loves for us to have joy too. That's just a glimpse of unconditional love. Dogs can demonstrate this kind of love so well.

2. **Forgiveness**: Even when we are "sticks in the mud" with our dog or maybe snap at them, they forgive us. They simply want to please us. They might even cuddle up next to us to say they are sorry or make us feel better. They don't look to blame, they just want you to be happy with them.

That's a true friend. Of course, this is a reciprocal act in this bonding friendship when your dog does something that might displease you.

When we do something that displeases God, we may be sorry and ask forgiveness, maybe spend some time in His word or in prayer. Jesus always forgives sincere repentance. Watching our dogs demonstrate this with us can help us better understand the power of forgiveness that Jesus offers. Of course, on a bit different scale.

3. Worship: I think dogs can even teach us a little bit about worship. The dog's world revolves around their "master." They trust them, honor them and obey or at least, try hard to obey. They gaze at their master with love and awe.

Oh my! If we as humans worshiped our Savior like a faithful dog worships us as their master, how many smiles would that put on our Master's face? Even without the tail wagging.

4. Joy: Dogs can teach us a thing or two about taking time to enjoy the simple pleasures of life. Watching your friend toss up a bug or a toy can put a smile on your face from northwest to northeast. You don't need any other source of entertainment. Or maybe joy comes in sharing a little tug play time or throwing a Frisbee. Maybe it is working side by side with your dog to bring some joy to someone else's life, like a child or maybe an elder in a nursing home. Animals in general and particularly dogs, can brighten someone's day in so many ways.

The importance your dog can play in, not only your own daily life, but also possibly another, should not be overlooked. If you have the opportunity, you might consider special training for your dog, so you and your dog can visit the elderly or possibly the disabled. Either way, dogs are a responsibility and do take a considerable time commitment, in most cases, for them to be a well behaved joy in your household. For this though, they give back to us in so many ways. Losing our dog friends can impact our life as much as losing our human friends. Cherish the joy you shared.

5. Friendship: It all can be summed up with friendship. There is no friendship like the one that can be shared with a loyal dog. Certainly, a true friend is a friend in good times or not so good times. And this works both ways. This is not always the case with some of the human friends we might have had through the years. I bet you have had people in your life, maybe even relatives, that claimed to be your friend, but proved to be the superficial fair weather human breed variety. Even a human dog friendship can be tested at times, maybe even on both sides, but with few exceptions, your 4-legged friend will still be your very best friend.

They daily show us how much they love us, forgive us and worship us. They can put a smile on our face just by looking at them. When your furry friend shares all this with you, it makes it easy to reciprocate this friendship. To show them how much we love them, we forgive them when they are a little naughty, cherish them as a dear friend, take care of them, train them and of course, give them a reason to smile when they look at us.

It is the ultimate of friendships as a true friend doesn't fault you, doesn't judge you and doesn't criticize you. A true friend is always happy to be with you, always happy to be your comfort, always happy to be your friend. Not sure too many people can boast a friendship like this with human counterparts, but it is certainly a model to strive toward.

Our dogs help us in so many more ways than what is listed above. For many, dogs fill deep emotional needs or very practical needs for those using dogs to help bridge the gap from certain disabilities or health conditions. They can even bring families closer together. They make great companions for the single person as well who may have bouts of loneliness. Dogs have certain skills and senses that make them a highly attuned companion on many levels.

Yes, I know, even the best of dogs can be annoying, but we love them anyway. No doubt, we annoy them sometimes, but they love us anyway.

I am assuming that you are reading this book because you have recently lost a cherished friend. Today, I want to offer hope that yes, you will see your beloved friend in heaven. Although painful to lose your friend, it is not the end of his or her life journey, it is just another step along the way. Your friend has "passed on" just as we all will some day. If your friend has "passed on"from earth, then he or she has had to pass onto somewhere else and that would be heaven.

In the pages ahead, I would like to share the compelling reasons why I feel you should be hopeful and not fret. Your friend is safe in heaven, happy and having fun while waiting for you, his master, to arrive as well. Of course, let's not forget your need to make sure that you will be there. If you are not sure, no worries, God makes this easy for you. Check out the next chapter.

ELVIS

I buried Elvis today
Eleven years ago he ambled onto our ranch
Weather-worn, tired, and hungry
Mostly looking for a friend

We almost didn't keep him
But something told me
This Aussie mix was special
So he joined our family

His instincts were strong
He ruled the roost
Herding horses, cats, and kids
And warning passers-by
This was his family, his territory

Unhappy memories sometimes surfaced
You could see it in his eyes
Perhaps scary nights alone in the forest
The cries of coyotes piercing the night

When frightened he'd hide under the deck
His dog cave of safety
Waiting for me the next morning
With his trademark woo-woo bark

Cancer got hold of him
Like so many other loved ones recently
We gave him eleven years of love
And he loved us back unconditionally

I buried Elvis today
In a spot that he loved
Where his spirit could be on-guard
His head pointed toward the forest
From which he came
I buried Elvis today...and sobbed

(© 2009 Bill Mintiens)

26

Chapter 2
How Do You Get To Heaven

From the beginning of time, God has loved you. You might not have been born yet, but he knew you were coming. He also knew that giving man a choice of whether he or she wanted to fellowship with their Creator or not, would have many choosing not. He knew that making man in His image and giving the gift of a free will would invariably have people reject Him.

Yet, He wanted a relationship with His creation, not something coerced or forced. Yet God is holy and as we sin or reject Him, it separates us more and more from Him. Still, He loved us. He mapped out a plan for human redemption, a Savior, Jesus Christ, His only son, who paid the price for our sin. Jesus bridges the gap between humans and our Heavenly Father. He even sent Jesus to earth to show us first hand how much He loves us, demonstrate His character and to reassure us that He has great compassion for His people.

Then being sinless, He willingly went to the cross to die for our sins once and for all. He did this in order that we could be in God's family through our Savior, Jesus. In 1 Cor 5:21, it says, God made him who had no sin to be sin for us, so that in him we might become the righteousness of God.

The story didn't end there. After dying on the cross for our sins, He rose again. He defeated death. He provides the way for us to have eternal life in God's family. This gift of salvation is for anyone who wants to accept this gift and truly wants Jesus to be the Lord of their life.

The most prominent and most quoted verse you can bank your life on is, John 3:16, "For God so loved the world that He gave His one and only son, that whosoever believes in Him, shall not perish, but have everlasting life." That's it. You don't have be perfect or "earn" your way into heaven. You just have to accept His gift of salvation and truly desire to live your life for and with Him.

Christianity is not really about religion or rules, but about a relationship, a relationship with our Lord and Savior, Jesus Christ. Be careful not to complicate this as so many do. And don't dismiss a relationship with your Savior because you know some people who "go to church" who aren't perfect. Perfection will not be found in anyone in this earthly life. Thankfully, God understands this and helps us along.

Romans 3:21-26 talks about the reconciliation Jesus provides and that our righteousness comes from him, not anything we can do, so no one can boast. "But now a righteousness from God, apart from the law, has been made known, to which Law and the Prophets testify. This righteousness from God comes through faith in Jesus Christ to all who believe. There is no difference, for all have sinned and fall short of the glory of God, and are justified freely by his grace through the redemption that came by Christ Jesus. God presented him as a sacrifice of atonement, through faith in his blood. He did this to demonstrate his justice, because in his forbearance he had left the sins committed beforehand unpunished–he did it to demonstrate his justice at the present time, so as to be just and the one who justifies those who have faith in Jesus."

Romans elaborates in 5:1-2, "Therefore, since we have been justified through faith, we have peace with God through our Lord Jesus Christ, through whom we have gained access by faith into this grace in which we now stand. And we rejoice in the hope of the glory of God."

Ponder on this, "For if, when we were God's enemies, we were reconciled to Him through the death of His son, how much more, having been reconciled, shall we be saved through His life! Not only is this so, but we also rejoice in God through our Lord Jesus Christ, through whom we have now received reconciliation." Romans 5:1-2.

Jesus said in John 14:6, "I am the way and the truth and the life. No one comes to the Father except through me." In Revelation 3:20 he says, "Here I am! I stand at the door and knock. If anyone hears my voice and opens the door, I will come in."

If you haven't accepted the gift of salvation that Jesus offers, but want to, the Bible tells us that we simply need to sincerely accept the gift. Romans 10:9 says, "If you confess with your mouth, 'Jesus is Lord,' and believe in your heart that God raised Him from the dead, you will be saved."

And these words so powerfully speak to the love God has ready to lavish on each of us, "To all who received Him, to those who believed in His name, He gave the right to become children of God." John 1:12.

When I try to comprehend just what it means to be a child of the Almighty God and to fully grasp all the details laid out throughout history, just so He could have a relationship with each one of us, it perplexes me. Yet, the Holy Bible lays out the evidence from the beginning of time. The only time-tested, eye witnessed accounts furnished for us.

Thank the Father above that we don't have to earn our way to heaven, as we all fall short. He knew this, but wanted us to be with Him forever as part of His family. He wants to have a relationship with each of us, His creation. And when we accept Jesus as Lord, the God's Holy Spirit connects with ours and then it goes beyond just the reading of the Bible, but you feel it in your spirit. It doesn't magically make everything easy on this earth, but you start to want to nourish a relationship with your Savior. As you do that, your friendship grows stronger and stronger. Your spirit entwines more and more with God's Holy Spirit and a peace that transcends all understanding takes hold. (Paraphrased from Philippians 4:7) More on that later.

To top it off, God's word tells us in Romans that nothing or no one can separate us from the love of God that is in Christ Jesus our Lord. If we want to know and love Him, we need to take that step toward Him. He has paved the way, but it is our choice whether to accept His invitation.

If you want to accept the gift of salvation that Jesus offers in order to reconcile yourself with your Heavenly Father, then you simply need to sincerely pray something like this.

Father God, I believe you love me. You sent Jesus to take away my sins and foolish ways. Through Jesus, I am reconciled to you, Father. I accept Jesus as my Lord and Savior. Help me to live my life in a way that pleases you. In Jesus name, Amen

It doesn't have to be these exact words. Pray from your heart. Once you have sincerely asked Jesus into your life, His Holy Spirit joins your spirit. It is as easy as that. "The Spirit of the Lord will come upon you in power, … and you will be changed into a different person." 1 Samuel 10:6

Follow that up with spiritual nutrition such as a Bible believing church, Bible study, a small group from your church and continual prayer, talking with God. Remember, your walk with the Lord is about a relationship with Him, not religious rules or man-made requirements.

Be aware that sometimes the binding Holy Spirit in our life clashes with our body or soul and it may pull on us in conflicting ways. That is why we must renew our minds daily to help us conform to God's Spirit. You can do that by simply talking with God, asking for His help, studying God's word and being part of a Bible believing church. As we do that, there is less clash and more harmony. It is truly a lifelong process, but you have a God that loves you and will help you along the way.

Here are some reassuring words for all of us, whether we just committed our lives to Jesus a couple moments ago or many years ago.

"I have loved you with an everlasting love." — Jeremiah 31:3 and "Indeed the very hairs of your head are numbered." — Luke 12:7

I will finish this chapter with this verse, "When I consider your heavens, the work of your fingers, the moon and the stars, which you have set in place, what is man that you are mindful of him, the son of man, that you care for him? You made him a little lower than the heavenly beings and crowned him with glory and honor." Psalm 8:3-5

Bottom line, God loves you and wants to have a relationship with you, forever, on earth and in heaven. So, now that you know you will be heaven, let's take a look at how the Bible tells us that your beloved pets will be there too.

"MONROE"

What a scared little creature that wandered off,
not able to hear the dangers around you,
nor the joys that could be yours.
Peace awaits you little girl.

"Wacky"

Doing what she does best, guarding and protecting. In this case, watching over the orphaned Jack Rabbits.

PART 1

WHY WOULDN'T THERE BE ANIMALS IN HEAVEN

"WATSON"

Some dogs have it pretty good and don't even know that in heaven, they'll have it even better ...

"BADGER"

What a silly boy!

Chapter 3
His Creation

The first hint that God's word gives us to establish that there will be animals in heaven is that He made animals before humans. And it was all part of His Garden of Eden. It was a garden of paradise and animals were included in it. Not only that, but animals are mentioned throughout many important events of history, including where Jesus was born. I think this alone indicates a strong probability that He will have animals in His heaven world as well.

Let me offer a human example to further illustrate why animals in heaven is a probable proposition, even without all the direct scriptures that tell us that there indeed are animals residing there. I'll use my wonderful mother as an example. She is a self-taught artist. She has created a variety of different paintings, but she has her favorite type of painting. She loves ocean or scenes with water in them. She is very good at them. Within that interest comes many different variations, but they all have water in them.

As a creator of art, she paints what she loves the most. If she loves to paint scenes with water and spends a great deal of thought and effort to do so, why would she not continue to create them? She wouldn't and she hasn't. She has painted water scene after water scene for the last 30 years. She had a guest in her house not too long ago and he described their house as aquatic. She has a water scene painting in literally every room of her house. She has surrounded herself with the created art she loves.

Wouldn't God want to do the same thing? Do you know how many species of animals exist? Neither do scientists know. They estimate that there are 3 to 30 million species of animals. Not to mention the variations that exist within the species. Why would He create millions of different species of animals for us on earth, but then not have any in heaven? It doesn't make sense that He wouldn't. The difference is that in heaven, as it was before the fall, when the Garden of Eden was actually paradise, all the animals live peacefully together. Now, that is something to look forward to.

Chapter 4
Animals Are Important To God

There are actually hundreds of animal references in the Bible that show the importance of animals to God. You are even more important and I will elaborate on why that is important to answering the question of whether your dog will be in heaven. For now, check out these key verses that indicate that there will indeed be animals in heaven. The inferences are numerous from Genesis to Revelation while at other times, very blatant. Here are just a few significant Bible references showing the importance of animals to God's creation.

God created the animals and said it was good. If God had changed His mind and no longer wanted animals as part of His creation, He could have let them all drown at the time of the flood, but He wanted them preserved.

God clearly shows us that animals are important to Him. He created every living creature in the sea and on the land and then He said it was "good." In Noah's day when everyone around was sinning and had turned away from God, God not only saved Noah and his family, but He wanted the animals to be saved as well.

God includes animals in His covenant spoken to Noah,

It is interesting that God included animals in His covenant at the time of the flood. He says, with every living creature of every kind and later in the passage, it says, all living creatures. Words like all and every means what it says. It doesn't say all living creatures except your pet dog. This passage in the Bible makes it very clear that God values not just some of His creatures, but all of His creatures, human or animal. Read Genesis 9:8-17. [Then God said to Noah and to his sons with him, "I now establish my covenant with you and with your descendants after you and with every living creature that was with you — the birds, the livestock and all the wild animals, all those that came out of the ark with you — every living creature on earth.

I establish my covenant with you: Never again will all life be cut off by the waters of a flood: never again will there be a flood to destroy the earth."

And God said, "This is the sign of the covenant I am making between me and you and every living creature with you, a covenant for all generations to come: I have set my rainbow in the clouds, and it will be the sign of the covenant between me and the earth. Whenever I bring clouds over the earth and the rainbow appears in the clouds, I will remember my covenant between me and you and all living creatures of every kind. Never again will the waters become a flood to destroy all life. Whenever the rainbow appears in the clouds, I will see it and remember the everlasting covenant between God and all living creatures of every kind on the earth."

So God said to Noah, "This is the sign of the covenant I have established between me and all life on earth."]

Again in Hosea, it speaks of a covenant including animals in heaven.

Hosea 2:18 "In that day I will make a covenant for them with the beasts of the field, the birds of the air and the creatures that move along the ground. Bow and sword and battle will abolish from the land, so that all may lie down in safety."

Sometimes His word flat out tells us that God saves humans and animals.

Psalm 36:6 tells us, "Your righteousness is like the mighty mountains, your judgments are like the great deep; you save humans and animals alike, O LORD." (NRS)

The NIV states it this way, "Your righteousness is like the mighty mountains, your justice like the great deep. O LORD, you preserve both man and beast."

"And the glory of the Lord will be revealed and all mankind together will see it." Isaiah 40:5 (NIV)

And how much clearer can it be, Luke 3:6 "all flesh shall see the salvation of God." (KJV)

These are just a few of the verses that tell us God saves the animals too. He tells us that ALL mankind will see the Lord's glory and all flesh the salvation of God. The Book of Genesis establishes clearly that animals have flesh and souls. It is obvious that animals have flesh as we can see that clearly, but Genesis also tells us that animals have souls. We will discuss this in a later chapter. For now, take comfort that God says ALL FLESH shall see the salvation of God.

Another similar and interesting Bible verse written by the wisest man on earth, Solomon, compares the fate of humans and animals.

Solomon, wrote this revelation in Ecclesiastes 3:19-21, "Man's fate is like that of the animals; the same fate awaits them both: As one dies, so dies the other. All have the same breath, man has no advantage over the animal. Everything is meaningless. All go to the same place; all come from dust and to dust all return. Who knows whether the spirit of man goes upward and the spirit of the beast goes down into the earth?" (NIV)

Although it appears Solomon's mood was a bit down at the time, it still highlights some interesting points that relate to our reassurance that animals and more importantly, our special dog friends will be in heaven.

1. Humans and animals live and die on earth, the same fate awaits us.
2. We both have the same breath, the breath of life as God clearly states in Genesis.
3. He understands that the animal has a spirit too. A subject we will expand upon in a later chapter.

He instructed us to rule over and take care of the animals. God puts the care of your animals above the law.

In Matthew 12:11, the Pharisees were trying to find a reason to accuse Jesus and they asked if it was lawful to heal on the Sabbath. Jesus said, "if any of you has a sheep and it falls into a pit on the Sabbath, will you not take hold of it and lift it out?" Then He goes on to answer with a human perspective. "How much more valuable is a man than a sheep! Therefore it is lawful to do good on the Sabbath."

Again in Luke 14:5. Jesus asks the Pharisees if it was lawful to heal on the Sabbath. They were silent. Then Jesus asked them, "if one of you has a son or an ox that falls into a well on the Sabbath day, will you not immediately pull him out?" And they had nothing to say.

God has used animals throughout the Bible to teach us in one way or another. Maybe the most well known example to bring home the point that animals are important to God is the passage in Matthew 6:26 where Jesus is trying to encourage us not to worry,

"Look at the birds of the air; they do not sow or reap or store away in barns, and yet your heavenly Father feeds them. Are you not much more valuable than they?"

Another similar one found in Matthew 10:29, "Are not two sparrows sold for a penny? Yet not one of them will fall to the ground apart from the will of your Father." (NIV)

Or how about this similar one in Luke 12:6 "Are not five sparrows sold for two pennies? Yet not one of them is forgotten by God."

A couple other verses that clearly teach us that animals are as much a part of God's plan as we are ...

"Ask the animals, and they will teach you...In God's hand is the life of every creature, and the breath of all mankind." (Job 12:7 and10)

"A righteous man cares for the needs of his animal." (Proverbs 12:10). This is an interesting verse on a few levels, but certainly shows how God wants us to care for our animals.

With many scripture references to the importance of animals in God's creation, the most significant relating to human redemption is that of the sheep and the shepherd. Interestingly, it is similar between master and dog.

The analogy of the sheep and the shepherd is used throughout the Bible. His teaching about this was for our (human) benefit, but it is interesting how He has used animals throughout His word to help us understand things.

I love the passages about how the sheep know their shepherd's voice in John 10. He used the sheep to make an analogy of how Jesus, the Shepherd, watches over His flock, (us). The way the shepherd tends and cares for his sheep is much like a dog owner cares for their dog. They look out for them, feed them and care for them. The sheep look to their shepherd, they know his voice and are in peace by his presence. So it is with our dogs. They look to us with admiration, know our voice and are most at peace when in our presence.

Certainly, one thing the Bible does tell us quite plainly is that animals are a huge part of God's creation.

It only makes sense that God would value that which He created, called good and used extensively throughout history. Food, sacrifice, redemption, wonder, instructing, studying, all to demonstrate an incredible Creator. For those of us who love dogs, He has allowed us to have adopted family members of sorts, which provide many of us with unconditional love, companionship, friendship, joy and much more. This isn't an accident.

This verse in Job 12:10 offers comfort on many levels. It should calm our spirits and put our minds at rest on this topic and any other for that matter,

"In His hand is the life of every creature and the breath of all mankind."

Animals play a significant role in helping people understand God's word in one way or another. Our pet dogs take that a huge step forward. Think about how your dog has enriched your life.

If you are fortunate enough to have your dog still with you, be sure to give them a hug now and then to thank them for all they give you. If you have lost a beloved friend, then take comfort that Jesus, who loves you, will love them in heaven.

It is my goal in writing this book, that I would give you hope that you will be reunited with your friend(s) in heaven. Let's now move onto the next chapter to look at further evidence that animals are in heaven .

Chapter 5
Animals Are A Shoe-In

Answering the question of whether animals will be heaven or not is the first step to bringing confidence to your spirit. If you are reassured that there will be animals in heaven, then why wouldn't your dog be there?

It is clear that animals have been a huge part of God's plan from the beginning of time as we touched on in the previous chapter. Before Jesus, animals were used to redeem us from sin for short periods of time. God allowed this form of sacrifice to cover sins, but in God's perfect garden, there was originally no need for this until man chose to sin. God is holy and there had to be some way for the people to cleanse themselves before God. That is, before Jesus came along to willingly take on the sins of the world once and for all, which provided the new way of being credited with righteousness.

Before the "fall" with Adam and Eve, animals and humans co-habitated peacefully. There wasn't any need for any form of redemption of sins as there wasn't any sin. We all know this was short lived, however, but it gives us a glimpse into what paradise might look like. So, before Jesus made the ultimate sacrifice, animals were used to temporarily redeem us from sin. But why animals? Maybe because they were without sin?

Sin is an issue of moral conscience and only humans have this. If you don't know something is a "sin," then technically you haven't "made the decision" to sin. Wild animals might do things we might consider mean, which interestingly only started after the "fall," but they don't actually sin.

Domesticated animals might misbehave, even willfully at times. They might know their master or owner wants them to obey a certain way and they choose not to. This is not sin though as they don't have this moral conscience.

The Bible tells us through old testament laws, as well as the 10 commandments, what was considered sin. If we, as humans, disobey those laws knowing they are considered a sin, then we have sinned. The purpose of the commandments and all those regulations were to basically enlighten us to what sin was, that we all fall short of the glory of God, and of course ultimately, to point us to our Savior, Jesus Christ, who was to come and now is.

So, if animals are considered sinless, wouldn't they go to heaven just on that point? That is, if you used the human redemption model, even though it is really irrelevant to the animal question. We do not have anything to indicate that it is the model God uses for this part of His creation. It simply doesn't relate. Irregardless, I have heard some people say that because they are "sinless," animals will be in heaven. Yet there are others who argue and say no, that animals don't have souls, so they can't go to heaven. (More on that coming up). There are many others who say the Bible's goal was to lay out the plan for human redemption, not animals, so there is no way to know what God's plan is for animals. All are reasonable opinions.

Indeed the Bible is to lay out God's plan for human redemption. He made man in His likeness, that is, to have a moral conscience, a free will, you might say. God went to a lot of planning to encourage a willing, reciprocal fellowship with Him and the humans He created. A plan that gives His human creation every opportunity to decide if we want to accept His gift of salvation and be part of God's family forever or not. He could have made us robots that worshiped Him, but instead He gave us a choice. He didn't want brainwashed robots, but a relationship with each of us. Sadly, many don't truly comprehend the magnitude of that or for whatever reason, have chosen not to believe or accept it.

Exactly where animals fit into this is a bit unclear, but we have established their importance in His plan. There are

44

actually many scriptures that tell us that there will be animals in heaven, but here are a few key ones.

One such reference that many people are familiar with is the scripture that tells us in Revelation that Jesus comes back riding a white horse. Some argue that this could be part of the symbolization of revelation. Either way, there are numerous other scriptures pointing to animals in heaven besides this one.

I shall repeat the verse that I used in a previous chapter as it tells us so authoritatively that animals will be heaven. Hosea 2:18 clearly says that humans and animals will peacefully co-exist. "In that day I will make a covenant for them with the beasts of the field, the birds in the sky and the creatures that move along the ground. Bow and sword and battle will abolish from the land, so that all may lie down in safety."

I love this part of scripture quoted from Romans 8:19-23 (KJV). It truly speaks to humans and animals being in this "fallen" world together, waiting for deliverance ... "For the earnest expectation of the creature waiteth for the manifestation of the sons of God. For the creature was made subject to vanity, not willingly, but by reason of him who hath subjected the same in hope. Because the creature itself also shall be delivered from the bondage of corruption into the glorious liberty of the children of God. For we know that the whole creation groaneth and travaileth in pain together until now. And not only they, but ourselves also, which have the firstfruits of the Spirit, even we ourselves groan within ourselves, witing for the adoption, to wit, the redemption of our body."

This verse tells us that animals are in the world's bondage as well, but they are waiting for their deliverance, which they will receive with the manifestation of the sons of God. It tells us that they will be delivered from this bondage into the glorious liberty of the children of God. Wow! Read that verse a few times, pray over it and ask God to help you fully grasp its wisdom. It quite blatantly tells us that animals became part of the consequences of the "fall," that they suffer and travel with us on this journey and that they too will be delivered from this bondage.

It is now time to tackle the big debate, which some people are quite confused about. The body, soul and spirit discussion. There are many that have trouble differentiating the definitions of the three. It can be a little challenging to grasp it completely and it may be that we will not fully understand until we meet the Lord face to face.

"NO NAME YET"

This puppy was found living in the landfill with its other siblings. Many feel that mistreated and orphaned dogs who didn't experience human friendship while on earth, will have homes in heaven, with people who didn't get to experience a canine friendship when living on earth.

Chapter 6
Body, Soul, Spirit

Let's begin with a few key references to the body (strength), soul (mind) and spirit (heart). In parentheses are meanings that sometimes are used interchangeably with body, soul and spirit. The word heart is used frequently in the Bible and usually refers to your spirit, the innermost part of who you are, truly the essence of body and soul.

Genesis 2:7 states that Man was created as a living soul. The soul consists of the mind (which includes the conscience), the will and the emotions. The soul and the spirit are intriguingly bound together and it is often referred to in scriptures as the "heart."

A scripture in the book of Proverbs declares, "Watch over your heart with all diligence, for from it flow the springs of life." (Prov. 4:23 NASB).

Dt 6:5 speaks of loving the LORD with all you are, "Love the LORD your God with all your heart and with all your soul and with all your strength."

Dt 10:12 "And now, O Israel, what does the LORD your God ask of you but to fear the LORD your God, to walk in all his ways, to love him, to serve the LORD your God with all your heart and with all your soul, and to observe the LORD's commands and decrees that I am giving you today for your own good."

Joshua 22:5 "But be very careful to keep the commandment and the law that Moses the servant of the LORD gave you; to love the LORD your God, to walk in all his ways, to obey his commands, to hold fast to him and to serve him with all your heart and all your soul."

There are countless scriptures that tell us how our body, soul and spirit interact. Scriptures that teach us how our spirit is the essence of who we are, more than just our personality, but the deepest, most inner you.

Your Body

The body is simply what we live in, so to speak. A container of sorts. It has all the parts needed to produce life, but whether alive or not, a body is still just a body. Think about it, a corpse is still a body with all the same parts as someone who is alive, yet the person is missing something that actually gives him or her life. You can lose parts of your body, but "you" are still alive. You are the same person, for example, whether you have legs or don't have legs or whether you are missing a finger or maybe an appendix. Irregardless of body size or shape, the body is still simply the container or tent that houses your spirit, that immaterial part of you that is the "real you," that which makes you a living soul.

Your Soul

The word soul is used over 850 times throughout the Bible. What is a soul? The answer to this gets taken out of context sometimes. Different cultures have different interpretations. Researchers, physicians and scientists, as well as Bible scholars, have added slight variations to the interpretation and definition of a soul, but the Bible states it clearly. The soul comes to being when you have the "breath of life." Your soul is your conscious being that includes your mind, feelings and will. Your soul basically exists so your spirit can function through the body.

Since the beginning of the Christian church, the most common understanding of living things has been that animals and humans have souls. Let's look at a few scriptures to set up a firm foundation and how the Bible makes it quite clear that this is so. Respected Bible scholars have confirmed this in various writings, commentaries and interviews. Not to mention, the clarity provided through certain scriptures throughout the Bible, from Genesis to Revelation.

Let us start at the beginning. In Genesis 2:7, it states, "And the LORD God formed man of the dust of the ground, and breathed into his nostrils the breath of life; and man became a living soul." (KJV), the NIV words it "... and the man became a living being." In the verses just prior to that, God talks about all the beasts of the earth, all the birds of the air and all the creatures that move on the ground as having the breath of life in it. This passage clearly indicates that the breath of life activates, if you will, our living being or soul, whether human or animal.

This "breath of life" is delivered to all our body cells via our blood. Without it, there is no life. It is like the fuel that moves your car from point A to point B and back to A. If you don't have gas in your car, it won't go. Similarly, your body won't function without the "breath of life," which makes the body a living soul or living being. In essence, it "turns you on" or gives you life, making you a living soul.

Having this breath of life brings life to our "mind," which has the ability to reason, make decisions and experience emotions. Your mind is more than your brain. Your brain has the incredible components that provide the opportunity to do these things, but like a computer, if you don't turn the switch on, the components are unused. We are born with the parts, but these "come alive" when we become a living being. BUT wait, there's more ...

Somehow and scientists still don't know exactly how, but when we become this living being, we become more than just parts. The same basic parts of anything will generally always come up with the same action or the same response to a particular situation. Not so with humans or animals as our soul or "mind" puts our own unique spin on things. You or I may face a nearly identical situation, but we may choose to react to it in totally different ways. Who we are, based on our experiences and thoughts related to those experiences will shape who we are deep in our soul. This makes each treasured soul different, whether human or animal.

How does your spirit fits into this? Keep in mind, I am talking about your dog too. So far, as you can see, it is clear that your dog has a soul as they have the breath of life in them. They experience emotions, make decisions and do reason things out on certain levels as do humans. We all have souls.

The Bible makes this clear right from the beginning in Genesis as well as clear scripture references all the way through the books of the Bible, all the way to the book of Revelation. Right in the very first chapter, Genesis 1:30, it tells us that the animals have the breath of life as well. "And to all the beasts of the earth and all the birds in the sky and all the creatures that move along the ground—everything that has the breath of life in it—I give every green plant for food."

Let's see how our spirits fit into who we are.

Your Spirit

The word spirit is used over 750 times in the Bible with about a third of that actually referencing to the Holy Spirit, which is different than your spirit. More on that in a later chapter.

Your spirit is the essence of who you are and is different than when we might say there was a spirit of anger in the room or spirit of joy, a quiet spirit or a spirit of timidity, etc. Sometimes we refer to an overall, collective essence of spirits of many or even a sixth sense if you will. We all put off energy and if we are intuitive, we can sometimes "feel" that energy. This may be referred to as a generalized feeling or spirit. (Dogs generally are very good at picking up on this energy). We can though have a part of this "spirit of anger or joy, etcetera," as part of our individualized spirit based on who we are as person or our approach to life and thought on a daily basis.

Your spirit, as many reputable Bible scholars describe, is basically the essence of who you are. It can be likened to a reflection of one's body and soul. It is the innermost you. It is the deepest part of you. Your spirit is eternal, it doesn't die. The Bible tells us that when our body dies, our spirit will return to God who gave it. "When Jesus himself died on the cross He said in a loud voice, "Father, into your hands I commit My spirit" When He had said this, He breathed His last. (Luke 23:46).

Your soul or mind can reason and make decisions as previously mentioned, but it is your spirit that really shapes those responses and emotions. It is your spirit that really directs your life response to the physical stimuli taken in by your body senses and thoughts that come into your soul/mind, because it is the innermost you, the essence of who you are. The soul and spirit are tightly connected, but are different.

The body houses your soul and spirit while on earth. Your body is a physical, tangible container for "you." Your spirit is the intangible "you" or "spiritual self." When your body dies on earth, your spiritual you, which is the reflection of your body and soul, is released to go back to God. Where you go from there is a whole different topic and depends on the choice you made on earth. (See chapter 2).

Your body or container will wear out or if it gets injured or ill, will weaken and/or eventually stop working. Think of a car. It is a container of parts like a human body. You fill it with fuel and it provides the energy to move it from here to there, but as your car ages, the parts eventually wear out. This may happen even quicker if it was in an accident or not maintained well. Your body, similarly, ages or wears out and eventually dies, but the essence of who you are or your spiritual self does not die, but moves on to be with the Lord for those who have accepted the gift of salvation through Jesus.

The body was made for life on earth, to contain our spiritual self while here. Here is a block of scripture,

51

1 Corinthians 15:35-54. It may help to explain the body, soul and spirit connection...

[But someone may ask, "How are the dead raised? With what kind of body will they come?" How foolish! What you sow does not come to life unless it dies. When you sow, you do not plant the body that will be, but just a seed, perhaps of wheat or of something else. But God gives it a body as he has determined, and to each kind of seed he gives its own body. All flesh is not the same: Men have one kind of flesh, animals have another, birds another and fish another. There are also heavenly bodies and there are earthly bodies; but the splendor of the heavenly bodies is one kind, and the splendor of the earthly bodies is another. The sun has one kind of splendor, the moon another and the stars another; and stars differs from star in splendor.

So will it be with the resurrection of the dead. The body that is sown is perishable, it is raised imperishable; it is sown in dishonor, it is raised in glory; it is sown in weakness; it is raised in power; it is sown a natural body; it is raised a spiritual body.

If there is a natural body, there is also a spiritual body. So it is written: "The first man Adam became a living being"; the last Adam, a life-giving spirit. The spiritual did not come first, but the natural, and after that the spiritual. The first man was of the dust of the earth, the second man from heaven. As was the earthly man, so are those who are of the earth; as is the man from heaven, so also are those who are of heaven. And just as we have borne the likeness of the earthly man, so shall we bear the likeness of the man from heaven.

I declare to you, brothers, that flesh and blood cannot inherit the kingdom of God, nor does the perishable inherit the imperishable. Listen, I tell you a mystery: We will not all sleep, but we will all be changed — in a flash, in the twinkling of an eye, at the last trumpet. For the trumpet will sound, the dead will be raised imperishable, and we will be changed. For the perishable must clothe itself with the imperishable, and the mortal with immortality, then the saying that is written will come true. "Death has been swallowed up in victory."]

1 Corinthians 15:35-54 clearly states that if there is a natural or physical body, whether human or animal, there is also a spiritual body. And it will be raised. This passage of God's word is one of the most comforting to bringing reassurance that our dog friends will be with us in heaven.

Our spiritual self, our dog included, will be released when our earthly body is done, along with our soul, which is basically what our spirit works through, that other immaterial part of you that is intangible, but what made you a living being.

The soul and spirit are tightly woven together as Hebrews 4:12 makes clear... "For the word of God is living and active. Sharper than any double-edged sword, it penetrates even to dividing soul and spirit, joints and marrow; it judges the thoughts and attitudes of the heart." (NIV).

An animal has a soul and their own spirit that shapes that soul. It is the essence of who they are. As in humans, their spirit reflects their body and soul. Isn't your spirit likened to your personality and your basic way of relating to circumstances and physical stimuli? Well, didn't each of your dogs in your life have their own personality? Didn't they have their own particular way of responding to things? Your soul is your intellect, will and emotions, but your spirit gives them life and personality. It is your innermost self. Without the interwoven spirit, your soul would basically be "lifeless"or at least a bit boring.

There are a variety of different scriptures throughout God's word that make it clear animals do have spirits. There is another verse that should help to clear the debate even further.

In the book of Numbers (16:22), the fourth book of the Bible, God was angry with some of the people who were rebelling against Moses and Aaron. Moses and Aaron pleaded for the innocent among the congregation. That doesn't relate, but what they said does. They call to God, the

God of the spirits of all flesh as stated in the King James Version and in the New International Version, it used the words all mankind. "But Moses and Aaron fell facedown and cried out, 'O God, God of the spirits of all mankind, will you be angry with the entire assembly when one man sins?'... 'O God, God of the spirits of all flesh' ..."   This verse clearly implies that humans and animals have spirits. It also connects the body or flesh to the spirit.

I used Ecclesiastes 3:18-21 in a previous chapter, but here it is again with the reminder that breath is often referred to as spirit, "As for humans, God tests them so that they may see that they are like the animals. Surely the fate of human beings is like that of the animals; the same fate awaits them both: As one dies, so dies the other. All have the same breath (literally "spirit"); humans   have   no   advantage   over   animals. Everything is meaningless. All go to the same place; all come from dust, and to dust all return. Who knows if the human spirit rises upward and if the spirit of the animal goes down into the earth?"

This scripture verse in Job 12:9-10 could sum up this whole book and even answer the question whether you will see your beloved dog in heaven. Speaking of our God Almighty, "In whose hand is the soul of every living thing, and the breath (spirit) of all mankind." (KJV) The NIV states it this way, "In His hand is the life of every creature and the breath (literally "spirit") of all mankind."

There are many references to animals having the "the breath of life" in them, the same wording attributed to humans. Animals, at different levels, all have the ability to think, reason and make decisions. Have you not called your dog before, "COME!" He or she looks at where they want to go, looks at you, then decides whether he shall obey or not. This is their will, their reasoning and decision making at work. Do you not have to have a soul and spirit for this?

I think the most blatant, clearest verse of hope is Corinthians 15:44, "it is sown a natural body, it is raised a spiritual body. If there is a natural body, there is also a

spiritual body." This tells us that every thing that has a
a natural body here on earth also has a spiritual body that is
eternal.

There is no doubt based on what the Bible does tell us, that
your dog has a body, soul and spirit. It also tells us that it will
be raised, but is that spirit different than ours?

"GLORY"

In honor and memory of the Wilcox's Jack Russel Terrier/Beagle mix who faithfully kept the mice at bay and truly brought glory to the Lord through their family bond and prayers related to her life's journey on this earth.

Chapter 7
How Our Spirit Differs From Animals

Our spirit is different from the animals, in at least one regard. "God said, 'Let Us make man in Our image, according to Our likeness; and let them rule over the fish of the sea and over the birds of the sky and over the cattle and over all the earth, and over every creeping thing that creeps on the earth.' God created man in His own image, in the image of God He created him; male and female He created them." (Genesis 1:26-27 NASB)

God made men and women to be a spiritual being like Him. Respected Bible scholars explain that this basically means that humans are made with a built in desire in their spirit to have meaningful fellowship with their Creator. It means that the human spirit is meant to be connected with God's Holy Spirit. We all know that not everyone chooses to make that connection, nevertheless, we are cable ready, so to speak. That is the most significant difference in our spirits. Of course, humans are capable of complex thoughts, but this cable ready spirit that men and women have make us the only living beings on earth, at least that we are aware of, who have the ability to relate to God intimately.

The Bible tells us that God took a handful of dust (which speaks of the earth), and He breathed life into it (which speaks of the spirit), and "man became a living soul" (Genesis 2:7, KJV). Thus, the merger of the spiritual with the physical elements of the earth created a human soul, made in the image of God.

The human spirit was made with the natural inclination to

fellowship with God's Holy Spirit, but a few have mistakenly confused the human spirit with God's Spirit. These are not the same. God provided a way to bridge the gap between man and His creation through Jesus. When we accept Jesus as our Savior, His gift to us for our salvation, the Holy Spirit connects with our spirit. It is by this grace from God that we are saved, not by works, so that no one can boast as stated in Eph 2:8. It doesn't necessarily mean that we are then perfect people as we still battle the flesh (body) with the different senses interacting with this fallen world. So, when Paul was explaining in the Book of Romans how he did what he did not want to do and what he did not want to do he did, he speaks of this battle between the earthly flesh we live in and the spiritual being we are that wants to please God. That is also what it means to work out our salvation or the renewing of our mind as we must rely on God, asking Him to help us make decisions that please Him.

There is no "spiritual" battle within an animal because their spirit does not have this same "cable ready hook-up" connection with God's Holy Spirit. God created the animals, but their spirit is not made in God's image, so they can't make moral decisions. Their spirit can choose right and wrong though, based on what they have been taught by us or what their environment has taught them.

Our pets may choose to obey or be willfully disobedient. Our human spirit makes those kinds of decisions all day long, doesn't it? So, although humans and animals have a conscience, humans have the additional moral conscience that relates to our Creator. The human spirit can very effectively squelch its moral conscience to point of apparent non-existence. Unfortunately, this is happening way too much these days.

In summary, we are different in that we can accept our Savior and receive the Holy Spirit, which comes to live in us with our spirit. Our dogs do not receive the Holy Spirit in this way.

The Holy Spirit is a deposit into our human spirit. Ephesians 1:13-14 says it guarantees salvation to all who believe. This is why a few claim this is the reason animals do not go to heaven, but this is applying the human redemption plan to animals, which is just not relevant.

It is important to understand that the Bible is like an instructional manual for human redemption as God made man in His image. He wants to fellowship with us, at least those of us who want to have a relationship with Him. He made animals to be part of this world and for man to take care of them, but we do not have a specific animal redemption manual. Technically, with what we know about human redemption, animals don't need redemption, at least not in the same way as us. Animals are not sinners. They don't know what sin is or isn't. They are not built with the cable ready hook-up connection to God's Holy Spirit. Yes, some might know what is right and wrong based on what we taught them, but that is not the same. People used animals for sacrifices to cleanse them of sins in the old testament. They did this because animals were considered sinless and were thought to be able to symbolically cleanse people of their sins, at least temporarily.

God created the whole universe with all the millions of animal species, plants and wonders, He can bring into heaven whatever He wants. We cannot impose our humanness on the animals because it just doesn't fit. What we know has to be from what truths God has revealed to us in His word. And God's word clearly mentions animals in heaven.

Knowing animals are in heaven is nice, but part 2 will provide scripture evidence that extends this reassurance to your beloved dog.

Tana Osborn

"SOCKS"

Our friendship grows ...

60

PART 2

WAITING FOR YOU IN HEAVEN

I hope that you are beginning to feel comforted that animals do exist in heaven, but that is only a start because really, who cares, if it doesn't include your trusted furry friend or friends. If you are convinced that there will be animals in heaven, then why wouldn't your dog be there too? That alone is the clincher. In the next few chapters, I'd like to provide you with unmistakable hope that allows you to confidently say,

"Until heaven then, my friend."

"SQUISHY"

I could not save you from your confusing past, but we spent good times together before your journey took you to heaven. What fond memories you leave with me. Until heaven then, my friend.

"Tayce"

Chapter 8
God Knows You And Loves You

Let us begin with just how much God wants to lavish you with His love. John 3:16 is one of the most quoted Bible verses. It sums it all up and makes it simple. "For God so loved the world that He gave His one and only son, that whosoever believes in Him shall not perish, but have everlasting life." God WANTS YOU to be in heaven with Him. He wants to lavish you with love. From the beginning of time as we know it, He has wanted to have a relationship with us. He made us "cable-ready" to connect with Him. Even though we messed it up multiple times throughout history and still do today, He wanted to provide us a way to be part of His family. Jesus is the way, truth and life for us, (John 14:6). He provided the Way, but it requires a choice from us. We either accept His gift of salvation or we don't.

Ephesians 2:4-5 says it nicely, "But because of His great love for us, God, who is rich in mercy, made us alive with Christ even when we were dead in our transgressions–it is by grace you have been saved."

With a gift of eternal salvation, wouldn't you be thankful and want to live your life in a way that pleases your Savior?

Ephesians 5:1-2 "Be imitators of God, therefore, as dearly loved children and live a life of love, just as Christ loved us and gave himself up for us as a fragrant offering and sacrifice to God."

In 2 Thessalonians 2:16-17, it reminds us of the eternal hope we have that although things can be difficult on earth, God will take care of us and it will all work out, some things on earth, but some things not until heaven. "May our Lord Jesus Christ himself and God our Father, who loved us and by His grace gave us eternal encouragement and good hope, encourage your hearts and strengthen you in every good deed and word." These are but a few of the encouraging, life giving words that we are given through God's word.

We are also told that He knit us together in our mother's womb and He knows our every thought, struggle and joy. Even the hairs on our head are numbered. He knows the days of our life. There is nowhere we can go where He is not. Because of His great love for you, whether you understand it or not, is HUGE. We are told His love is beyond complete human comprehension. Using a puny human example, think about someone you unselfishly love and cherish. Maybe a parent, child, friend or even a pet. If there was something that was really important to them, something that filled their life with joy and was good for them, would you not want to provide that for them forever? This is such a minuscule example, but multiply that feeling as many times as possible in your mind and even then, the Bible tells us that it doesn't compare to how much God loves you and the plans He has for you.

In Jim Daly's article, Mr. Daly writes" A man once asked Dr. Billy Graham whether his dog would go to heaven. The great evangelist answered:

"God will prepare everything for our perfect happiness in heaven, and if it takes my dog being there, I believe he'll be there."

Whatever we consider to be a joy here on earth will be heightened millions of times beyond anything we can conceive when we get to heaven. The apostle Paul put it this way: "However, as it is written, No eye has seen, no ear has heard, no mind has conceived what God has prepared for those who love Him" (1Corinthians 2:9).

We are reassured that heaven will be more wonderful than we can imagine. Even what we can imagine has to be infinitely better than what this earth has become. But it is because of God's knowledge of who you are, what you cherish and how much He loves you, that I believe your beloved dog friend(s) will be reunited with you in heaven.

(I also believe your relationship will be sweeter than it once was and maybe even with a twist, which I'll explain in a later chapter).

Paul's letter to the Ephesians (3:18-19) praying that they "...may have power, together with all the saints, to grasp how wide and long and high and deep is the love of Christ, and to know this love that surpasses knowledge–that you may be filled to the measure of all the fullness of God." I like the rest of it too, (3:20). "Now to him who is able to do immeasurably more than all we ask or imagine, according to his power that is at work within us, to him be glory in the church and in Christ Jesus throughout all generations, for ever and ever! Amen."

Nothing can separate us from His love...

Romans 8:37-39 "No, in all these things we are more than conquerors through Him who loved us. For I am convinced that neither death nor life, neither angels nor demons, neither the present nor the future, nor any powers, neither height nor depth, nor anything else in all creation, will be able to separate us from the love of God that is in Christ Jesus our Lord."

All God has chosen to reveal to us points us and encourages us to accept Him as our Creator, but why does He do this? He does this because He wants to have a relationship with you. All He has shown, in a sense, is about the desire for this connection. The whole universe appears to be about His desire to have a relationship with each one of us. Each one of us is born unique, our own container labeling fingerprint, if you will, as well as a special living spirit that gives life to our soul. He loves each of us for who we are and wants to have a relationship with us. Can you even imagine the enormity of that? The Creator of the universe, the Almighty God wants to have a relationship with YOU.

Of course, He is holy and we fall short of the glorious and powerful Almighty God. That's why Jesus came, to bridge this gap, to reconcile us to God, the Father.

65

Jesus came and showed us more about God's compassionate character and then became the way, truth and life for us, our Savior, that allows us to forever be in God's family. God did all this for YOU. Why? Because He wants you in His family. He wants you to live with Him forever. He gave you the ultimate gift. You decide if you want to receive it.

I agree with Billy Graham, "*God will prepare everything for our perfect happiness in heaven, and if it takes my dog being there, I believe he'll be there.*" But I think this can be taken a bit further. If in your spirit, you want to be with your beloved dog friends even when in heaven, then the God who loves you and knows your heart will make this happen, won't He?

Remember, your spirit is the essence of who you are and that same spiritual "body" will be released to go to heaven when your body dies. Wouldn't the desire to be reunited with your pets still be present? Of course it would as your spirit is the "real you." It is the essence of who you are and you will still be "you" when brought up to heaven.

Wouldn't you rejoice over seeing Jesus, your human loved ones as well as your treasured dog(s) that you loved so dearly on earth? God has gone to a whole lot of trouble and planning to demonstrate His love for you, so, I believe your perfect happiness will indeed include your beloved furry friends if that is the desire of your spirit.

God knows you and the desires of your heart. His word tells us that there will be no sorrow in heaven. There would be great sorrow for me if my beloved furry friends were not with me for eternity. God knows this and will not allow that sorrow. It is because of God's love for you and I and His knowledge of our heart that reuniting us with our beloved pets in heaven is an unquestionable reality.

Chapter 9
God Loves To Give Us Good Gifts

Having a dog that you strongly connect with is a gift in itself. This connection can vary depending on personalities, just like our human friends. There are certain spirits we tend to connect closer with, but each one is special and truly a gift.

"The dog is the most faithful of animals and would be much esteemed were it not so common. Our Lord God has made his greatest gift the commonest." Martin Luther

The Bible tells us that perfect gifts come from above in James 1:16-18, "Don't be deceived, my dear brothers. Every good and perfect gift is from above, coming down from the Father of the heavenly lights, who does not change like shifting shadows. He chose to give us birth through the word of truth, that we might be a kind of firstfruits of all he created."

If God planned all of history to give us ample opportunity to choose whether we wanted to be with Him forever and provided the Way, wouldn't He also know how to give other good gifts?

God knows how to give good gifts. Matthew 7:9-11 makes a point of encouraging us regarding this, it states, "Which of you, if his son asks for bread, will give him a stone? Or if he asks for a fish, will give him a snake? If you, then, though you are evil, know how to give good gifts to your children, how much more will your Father in heaven give good gifts to those who ask him!" He knows how to give good gifts and that is another reason why God would want to reunite you with your beloved pets in heaven.

Of course, who can deny the greatest gift as Romans 6:23 tells us, "For the wages of sin is death, but the gift of God is eternal life in Christ Jesus our Lord."

Do you think God will stop giving you gifts when you get to heaven? No, the Bible says our joy in heaven will be more than we could ever imagine.

For many of us, next to our human family, wouldn't the best gift be our dog friends? God knows and cares about our heart. He is on our side through the good and not so good in life. And although we don't understand everything, we are taught to trust Him.

For whatever reason your dog has left you from your earthly home, God knows your loss and some day you will understand. Share your grieving pain with the Lord who loves you. Let Him comfort you and reassure you that your beloved dog is being cared for in heaven until it is your turn to come, then, what a wonderful reunion that will be.

Here are a few more reassuring verses from the Psalms that tell us that God loves all He has made. That includes His animals, which of course, includes your pets.

Psalm 145:8-10 "The Lord is gracious and compassionate, slow to anger and rich in love. The Lord is good to all; he has compassion on all he has made. All you have made will praise you, O LORD; your saints will extol you."

Psalm 145:13 ..."The LORD is faithful to all his promises and loving toward all he has made."

Psalm 145:16-17 "You open your hand and satisfy the desires of every living thing. The LORD is righteous in all his ways and loving toward all he has made."

Psalm 145:21 ..."Let every creature praise his holy name for ever and ever."

God loves all He has made, especially you, and He loves to give good gifts. Take comfort for that reason, as well as others, that you can be realistically hopeful that you will be reunited with your friend(s) in heaven.

He knows how you treasured these living souls He created, how you adopted them into your family and the friendship you shared with them. God loves you and He knows how to give good gifts. He will make sure they are taken care of until it is your turn to be brought up to heaven. Then you can watch over them once again.

"Wilson"

I am sure in heaven,
your job will involve running and howling.
That's doing what you love
and loving what you're doing.

Chapter 10
Your In Charge

The animals, including your pets, are all part of His creation. In many verses, including the ones previously mentioned, His word tells us that God has compassion on ALL He has made. He gave us the breath of life that made us a living soul with a spirit that makes us who we are. He did the same for your dog. This is all from God. Do you think it surprises Him that some peoples' spirits bond strongly to some dogs? This is all part of His creation. All part of the wonders of this life. And you are in charge of these little awesome creatures. When you brought that dog home, you vowed to take care of it, to love it and forge a loving relationship with him or her, even though it would require a lot of work. There are countless references to work in the Bible. It is obvious that God uses work to help our character and to offer service to others.

In Colossians 3:23-24, it says "Whatever you do, work at it with all your heart, as working for the Lord, not for men, since you know you will receive an inheritance from the Lord as a reward. It is the Lord Christ you are serving."

Work, whatever it entails, serves us and others on many levels. The Bible indicates that we will not be sitting around in heaven having nothing to do. We will have work there too. Not like human work that is often filled with stress, pressure and workplace drama, but enjoyable work. Our work will be joyful. Work that may include interests, hobbies or things we didn't get to do on earth. Irregardless of what it is, we know we will enjoy it.

I believe our pets will be able to be part of our work in some way. For me, I have this vision of working a carefree "heavenly" garden with my wonderful 4 legged friends at my side, maybe running through the rows of corn laughing and playing, those friends that I was so privileged to be a "master" to on earth.

God's word tells us that humans are in charge of the animals. Owning a dog puts us directly in charge of a particular doggie soul. It becomes our responsibility to take care of them and truly they become more than friends, but family. God knows our hearts. I believe our investment and work we have put into our dogs will be rewarded, both on earth and in heaven, both for us and them.

"Hunter"

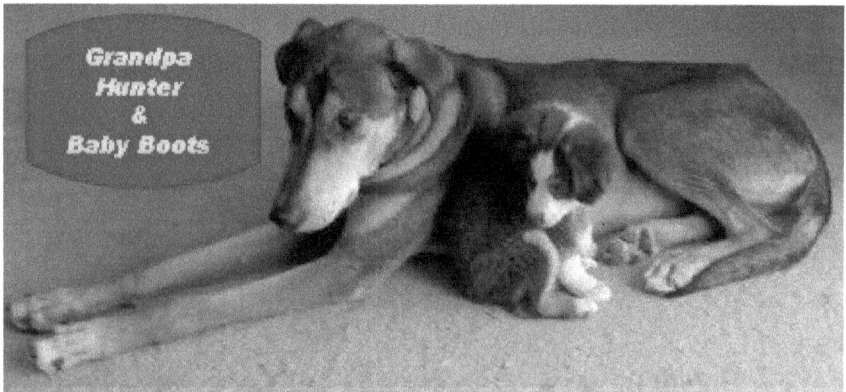

Grandpa Hunter & Baby Boots

A special friend with a kind spirit. Until heaven then, Hunter, when we see you again.

Chapter 11
Your Dog Is Covered

In chapter 6, many irrefutable scripture references were provided that clearly tell us that animals have a soul and spirit along with their body or flesh type. The animal flesh is different, but like human flesh, it is still just the container for our spirit, which makes each of us a living soul. Although the human spirit was created differently, in that, it was made with the ability to connect with the Holy Spirit, the animal spirit is still the essence of who the animal is. It is a reflection of their body and soul. When they die, that immaterial part of them lives on, returning to God.

The Bible was written to teach us about God's relationship and plan for people, but if we are paying attention for the mention of animals, it does tell us that animals go to heaven. It does tell us that animals have a body, soul and spirit and that God has compassion on every living thing. Job 12:9-10 says this about our Heavenly Father, "In whose hand is the soul of every living thing, and the breath (spirit) of all mankind." (KJV) The NIV states it similarly, "In his hand is the life of every creature and the breath of all mankind." That pretty much covers humans and animals, every creature that has breath.

Here is another one, Psalm 36:6 "Your righteousness is like the mighty mountains, your judgments are like the great deep; you save humans and animals alike, O LORD." (NRS)

"Be thou comforted, little dog, Thou too in Resurrection shall have a little golden tail." Martin Luther

73

If animals are saved, then that includes your dog(s). AND wouldn't He reunite you with those pets that you yearn so deeply to be with again? I think so. I believe the Bible gives us ample reason to have hope in that. Even if for some reason God had some other plan, when you get to heaven you will fully understand and your joy will be great.

It is because of what the apostle Paul said in 1 Corinthians 2:9 and many other verses like it, that I am 100% convinced that our beloved pets will be reunited with us in heaven. "No eye has seen, nor ear has heard, no mind has conceived what God has prepared for those who love Him." (I Corinthians 2:9).

We must trust the Lord. All will be more wonderful than we can imagine. What else does God's word tell us about heaven that indicates our beloved dogs will be there?

CHAPTER 12
What We Know Of Heaven

Animals And Humans Finally At Peace

In Isaiah 11:6-9, we catch a glimpse of what the world will be like after Jesus returns: "The wolf also shall dwell with the lamb, the leopard shall lie down with the young goat, the calf and the young lion and the fatling together; and a little child shall lead them. The cow and the bear shall graze; their young ones shall lie down together; and the lion shall eat straw like the ox. The nursing child shall play by the cobra's hole, and the weaned child shall put his hand in the viper's den. They shall not hurt nor destroy in all My holy mountain, for the earth shall be full of the knowledge of the LORD as the waters cover the sea."

In that day there not only will be lasting love and fellowship among the people of the earth but also, according to the prophet, among the animals as well! How wonderful!

Animals Wait For Their Deliverance

God's word also tells us in the book of Romans that even the creature waits to be delivered from the bondage of this corrupted world. They are subjected because of us. Here is that verse again, "For the earnest expectation of the creature waiteth for the manifestation of the sons of God. For the creature was made subject to vanity, not willingly, but by reason of him who hath subjected the same in hope. Because the creature itself also shall be delivered from the bondage of corruption into the glorious liberty of the children of God." Romans 8:19-21 (KJV).

We are to rule over the animals. They are in our dominion. So certainly, it makes sense that they are subjected to the things of this world while they wait for people to be redeemed as the children of God. They often suffer the consequences for the sins of humans. They will be delivered as well.

Good news for so many animals that have been mistreated and abused. And certainly good news for those loving pets that have brought so much life and joy to our hearts.

We Have Special Things Awaiting Us

A commentary written to describe heaven says that whatever we consider to be a joy here on earth will be heightened millions of times beyond anything we can conceive when we get to heaven. The apostle Paul put it this way: "Eye has not seen, nor ear heard, nor have entered into the heart of man the things which God has prepared for those who love Him" (I Corinthians 2:9).

We are reassured that being in heaven will bring us peace and joy beyond anything we could even dream up here on earth. All the pain and chaos from living in this fallen world will be gone. Revelation 21:3-4 tells us, "He will dwell with them, and they shall be His people, and God Himself will be with them and be their God. And God will wipe away every tear from their eyes; there shall be no more death, nor sorrow, nor crying; and there shall be no more pain, for the former things have passed away."

Recognizing Loved Ones

Our spirit is the essence of our soul and body that we lived in on earth. Our spirit will be recognizable in heaven, even before we get our resurrected bodies. To be assured of this, remember in the Book of Matthew when Jesus went up on the mountain with Peter, James and John and met with Moses and Elijah, who came from heaven. We are told that Peter recognized them.

I would like to share something that happened to me while working as a nurse in a long term care center. Being a nurse and a paramedic prior to becoming a nurse, I have been present with many people taking their last breath.

One day, I was caring for an elderly lady who was nearing her last moment on earth. I was tending to her when she took her final breath. At the instant she took her last breath, I saw, what I believe must have been her spirit leaving her body. It was only a fraction of a second that I was privileged to witness this. She was definitely recognizable. The best way I can describe it is that it was sort of like those holograph images you see portrayed on television. It looked just like her and she had the most awesome expression of peace on her face. Why I was allowed to see that, I may not know until I get to heaven to ask Jesus face to face. I am thankful as it has given me reassurance that death from this earth is just a step along the way in our life journey. I believe it is the same with our doggie friends.

So yes, there will be great elation over seeing our loved ones in heaven. There is no reason to ponder whether our pets will be recognizable as well because their spirit is also the essence of their soul and body in which they lived in on earth. God's word tells us this throughout the Bible. The Word tells us that if there is a physical body, there is also a spiritual body and it will be raised. (1Corinthians 15:44).

God has prepared a truly "heavenly" place for us and our beloved dogs. He has us in the palm of His hand. We will understand all the things we couldn't make sense of on earth once we get there. Communication will be better and love perfected, so we truly will be better people. I wouldn't be surprised if Jesus had all my beloved pets that have gone before, lined up ready to greet me when I and my other pets arrive at the pearly gates.

In my heart and in your heart, you can confidently say to each of your beloved dog friends, "Until heaven then my friend, when I see you again."

"WACKY"

Our friend and protector...

PART 3

INTERESTING POSSIBILITIES
"What Do You Think?"

"Moose"

If dogs could pray,
what do you think
they would pray for?

Chapter 13
Conversation For The Birds

Revelation 19:17-18 describes a scene that will happen during the end times. John is explaining what he saw in revelation, And I saw an angel standing in the sun, who cried in a loud voice to all the birds flying in midair, "Come, gather together for the great supper of God ..." The angel was telling them they could feed on the all the evil kings, mighty men, etc, that were about to be destroyed, which is irrelevant to my point. What is interesting is that he spoke to the birds and they understood.

Revelation 8:13 speaks of an eagle calling out to the inhabitants of the earth. There are other scattered references to animals having greater understanding in heaven.

Another interesting verse is in Isaiah 11:9 that says "They shall not hurt nor destroy in all My holy mountain, for the earth shall be full of the knowledge of the LORD as the waters cover the sea." This seems to imply that even the animals will have a deeper understanding or knowledge of the LORD.

This opens up wonderful possibilities for you and your beloved dog when you are reunited in God's new earth or kingdom.

So, in heaven, will our communication and understanding of each other be enhanced? Some intriguing possibilities to ponder on.

Hmmm!

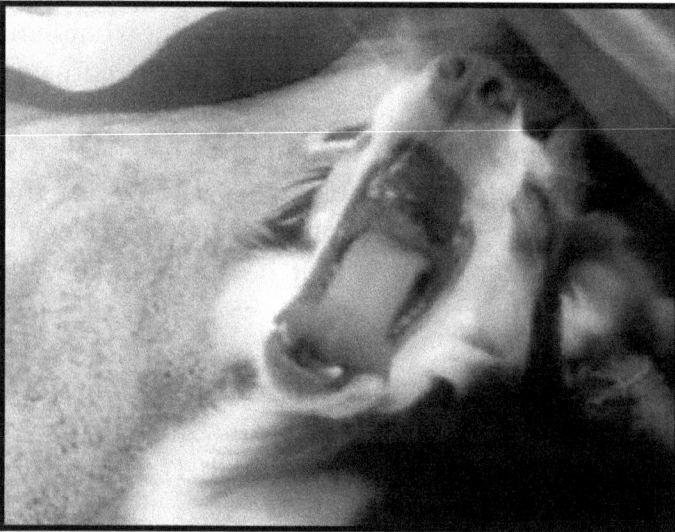

Dogs talking human
gets the imagination going.

Chapter 14
Talking Human

I think the story of Balaam's donkey in the book of Numbers presents fascinating possibilities. Some speculate that God spoke through the donkey while others say God gave the donkey the ability to speak. You can decide. Either way still makes you wonder what our dogs might be able to do in heaven.

I won't get into the whole story that led up to the donkey talking, but basically, Balaam was asked to go to Balak and tell the people something. First, he was in rebellion against the Lord, going to Balak for his own purposes and not those of the Lord. Second, the donkey's refusal to continue down the path enraged him so he beat her out of his anger because she had mocked him and made a fool of him, in his opinion. Anger has a way of curtailing rational thought, and perhaps he was so intent on exerting his dominance over the animal that he lost the ability to think clearly. It wasn't until the angel opened Balaam's eyes to see reality that he relented in his anger against the donkey, listened to the angel, and repented.

Here it is in a little more detail

Balak, king of Moab, was afraid of the Israelites that came to Moab. They had just conquered the Amorites. He sent for Balaam to come put a curse on the people. God told Balaam not to go saying the Israelites were blessed. Balak sent others to convince Balaam. Balaam said he couldn't do anything big or small that went beyond the command of the Lord, but said he would inquire as to what else the Lord might tell him. The next morning, the Lord said he could go, but he needed to do only what He told him. Further notes on why the Lord said he could go indicate that Balaam didn't have pure intentions and God was angry with him.

Then it starts to get a little intriguing. So, Balaam gets on his donkey and goes with the princes of Moab. Riding along with his two servants with him, an angel of the Lord appears on the path just ahead of them with drawn sword in hand. Balaam doesn't see the angel of the Lord, but the donkey does.

The donkey sees the angel of the Lord with drawn sword to strike Balaam down. The donkey veers off the road and goes into a field. Balaam, oblivious, beats the donkey to get back on the road. Later when on a narrow path between two vineyards and walls on both sides, the angel of the Lord appears again. The donkey presses close to the wall, which crushes Balaam's foot. He beats the donkey again.

A third time where there was no place to turn around and the angel of the Lord appears again, the donkey again tries to save Balaam and lays down. He beat her again.

Then we are told, the LORD opened the donkey's mouth, and she said to Balaam, "What have I done to you to make you beat me these three times?"

Balaam answered the donkey, "You have made a fool of me! If I had a sword in my hand, I would kill you right now."

The donkey said to Balaam, "Am I not your own donkey, which you have always ridden, to this day? Have I been in the habit of doing this to you?"

"No," he said.

Then the LORD opened Balaam's eyes, and he saw the angel of the Lord standing in the road with sword drawn. So he bowed low and fell facedown.

The angel of the Lord asked him, "Why have you beaten your donkey these three times? I have come here to oppose you because your path is a reckless one before me. The donkey saw me and turned away from me these three times. If she had not turned away, I would certainly have killed you by now, but I would have spared her."

The story continues with Balaam having more of an obedient heart toward God. For a while.

The story gives us some eyebrow raising things to ponder.

Raised eyebrow #1-the donkey, part of God's creation, was allowed to see the angel, not just once, but three times.

In heaven, will our dog be more attuned to the knowledge of God?

Raised eyebrow #2-Balaam has a conversation with the donkey.   That means, at the very least, the donkey understood, reasoned and articulated her thought out loud. Balaam answers his donkey like he is not surprised the donkey is talking to him. Maybe because he is in a fit of anger or having a temper tantrum and it doesn't really register that his donkey is talking to him. We aren't really told.

In heaven, will we be able to have actual verbal conversations with our dog?

Raised eyebrow #3-God allowed the donkey to speak. For whatever reason He chose to use the donkey this way, which to me, is irrelevant. The fact is He did. It opens up the imagination of possibilities. It is not the only time in scripture that describes an animal speaking either.   In Revelation 8:13, the word tells us that an eagle called out to the inhabitants of the earth.

In heaven, will He give animals the ability to speak "human?"

They may understand more than we know...

I strongly believe and research confirms that dogs are way more intelligent than many give them credit. Of course, we all know and maybe have owned dogs that might question that statement at times, but it is no different with us humans, right? Although they don't have the same reasoning powers or brain complexity as a human, generally speaking, they understand a great deal.

They also have an unusual sense of intuitiveness. They may not be able to verbally articulate their thoughts in human words, but they still think and respond to their world accordingly. Their senses are generally stronger than ours and they can pick up subtle vibes in their surrounding environment, seemingly like extrasensory perception at times.

And just because dogs don't "talk" in words like us, doesn't mean they don't communicate. Indeed they communicate quite effectively sometimes. Maybe it is a bark to be let outside. A nip at the heel to get us to go somewhere. A lick on the hand just to say I am glad you are my owner and friend. It is the snuggling up next to us when we are not feeling well. Maybe the warning an especially intuitive dog can give a diabetic that they are about to have a diabetic episode. Maybe a happy tail wagging walk in the park with you to express their happiness.

Our dogs communicate plenty if we are listening. They might not understand all our words, but neither do humans. Over time, we learn the meaning of the words in our world. Even as infants and toddlers, we can't formulate intelligible words, but in time, it happens. If we go to a foreign country, the language might be completely different. Communication might be difficult at times, but you would find ways to communicate, verbally or non-verbally. It is similar to this with our dogs. It is sort of like two "people" that speak two different languages living together. You learn to communicate successfully with each other despite the differences.

In heaven, will we have heightened conversation ability with our beloved furry friends? Something to ponder. I find the possibility exciting. Remember that God can do anything. We often put limits on God, but when you stop to think about the incredibleness of His creation, you might be reminded of His words ...

"I am the Lord, the God of all mankind. Is anything too hard for me?" — Jeremiah 32:27

Chapter 15
What Does The Lord Tell You

God tells us that we will be made perfect in heaven and we will understand all those things we can't even begin to fully grasp here on earth. Paul writes in 1 Cor. 13:12, "Now we see but a poor reflection as in a mirror; then we shall see face to face. Now I know in part; then I shall know fully, even as I am fully known." The many things we don't fully understand here on earth will become clear when in heaven. For now, we simply must trust the Lord, as best we can, until that day when all becomes clear.

There are joys and sorrows in our earthly life, but He tells us that there will be no more sadness or pain in heaven, so trust Him. In this book, I have provided some of the more obvious verses that were written down in God's word that, I believe, clearly tell us that animals, more specifically, your beloved dog friend(s) will be with you in heaven.

I hope this book has brought a calming reassurance that the Lord is taking care of your friend(s) in heaven and that you will be reunited with them when it is your time to do so. I encourage you to firm up your hope and reassurance by talking with the Lord, if you haven't already. Express to Him the pain you feel about losing your beloved friend. Let Him speak to you through His Holy Spirit within you. Let Him reassure you. The vastness of the universe He created is beyond our grasp, yet as splendorous as all of that might be, His most treasured creation is YOU. He knows the number of your days, He knows your thoughts before you think them and every hair on your head. He knows your heart and love for your dog(s). Let Him comfort your spirit like no one else can.

Let His peace that transcends all understanding consume your grief and help you to move forward in your life. Although this life may not be easy sometimes, God is there with you and somehow it will all make sense when we get to heaven.

For now, take comfort that His word clearly tells us that animals will be in heaven and that God knows and cares about the desires of your heart. Even though you now miss your wonderful dog(s) that have gone to be with the Lord, you can say confidently, "Until Heaven Then, My Friend," as you know in your heart, you will see them again.

Notes

Scripture taken from the Holy Bible, New International Version, NIV, unless otherwise indicated. Copyright 1973,1978, 1984 by Biblica, Inc. Used by permission of Zondervan. All rights reserved worldwide.

Holy Bible, King James Version, KJV. Copyright 1972 by Thomas Nelson, INC.

Various scriptures used throughout including those below.

Chapter 1

1. 1 Chronicles 16:29
2. 1 John 1:9
3. Isaiah 55:12
4. John 15:11
5. 1 Thessalonians 2:19
6. Philemon :7
7. Proverbs 17:17

Chapter 2

1. Acts 2:22-28
2. Colossians 1:15-23
3. Colossians 2:9-15
4. Matthew 1:21
5. John 1:29
6. Romans 6:22-23
7. 2 Corinthians 5:11-21
8. Matthew 28:1-10
9. John 20
10. Ephesians 1:8-9
11. Ephesians 2:4-10
12. Romans 5:5
13. Romans 5:8-10
14. Romans 8:28-39
15. 1 Corinthians 5:21
16. John 3:16
17. Romans 3:21-26
18. Romans 5:1-2
19. John 14:6
20. Revelation 3:20
21. Romans 10:9
22. John 1:12
23. Philippians 4:7
24. 1 Samuel 10:6
25. Jeremiah 31:3
26. Luke 12:7
27. Psalm 8:3-5

Chapter 3
1. Genesis 1:20-25

Chapter 4
1. Genesis 1:20-25
2. Genesis 7:1-3
3. Genesis 9:8-17
4. Hosea 2:18
5. Psalm 36:6
6. Psalm 36:6 (NRS)
7. Isaiah 40:5
8. Luke 3:6 (KJV)
9. Ecclesiastes 3:19-21
10. Matthew 12:11
11. Matthew 6:26
12. Matthew 10:29
13. Luke 14:5
14. Job 12:7
15. Job 12:10
16. Proverbs 12:10
17. John 10
18. Luke 12:6

Chapter 5
1. Genesis 2
2. Romans 13:5
3. Hebrews 10:22
4. 1 Peter 3:16
5. Exodus 20
6. Revelation 6:2
7. Hosea 2:18
8. Romans 8:19-23
9. Romans 8:19-23 (KJV)

Chapter 6
1. Genesis 2:7
2. Genesis 2:7 (KJV)
3. Proverbs 4:23 (NASB)
4. Deuteronomy 6:5
5. Deuteronomy 10:12
6. Joshua 22:5
7. Genesis 1:30
8. Luke 23:46
9. 1 Corinthians 15:35-54
10. Hebrews 4:12
11. Numbers 16:22
12. Numbers 16:22 (KJV)
13. Ecclesiastes 3:18-21
14. Job 12:9-12
15. Job 12:9-12 (KJV)
16. 1 Corinthians 15:44

Chapter 7
1. Romans 7:21-25
2. Romans 12:2
3. Ephesians 1:13-14
4. Genesis 1:26-27 (NASB)
5. Genesis 2:7 (KJV)

Chapter 8
1. Ephesians 1:7-8
2. 1 John 3:1
3. John 14:6
4. Psalm 139:13-18
5. Psalm 139
6. Matthew 10:30
7. Psalm 40:5
8. Psalm 37:4
9. Psalm 103:1-5
10. Jeremiah 31:12-13
11. Revelation 7:17
12. John 3:16
13. Ephesians 2:4-5
14. Ephesians 5:1-2
15. 2 Thessalonians 2:16-17
16. 1 Corinthians 2:9
17. Ephesians 3:18-20
18. Romans 8:37-39

Chapter 9
1. Romans 6:23
2. Ephesian 2:8
3. James 1:16-18
4. Matthew 7:9-11
5. Romans 6:23
6. Psalm 145:8-10
7. Psalm 145:13
8. Psalm 145:16-17
9. Psalm 145:21

Chapter 10
1. Hebrews 6:10
2. Colossians 3:23-24

Chapter 11
1. Proverbs 3:5-6
2. Job 12:9-10
3. Job 12:9-10 (KJV)
4. Psalm 36:6 (NRS)
5. 1 Corinthians 2:9

Chapter 12
1. Isaiah 11:6-9
2. Romans 8:19-21 (KJV)
3. Revelation 21:3-4
4. 1 Corinthians 2:9

Chapter 13
1. Revelation 19:17-18
2. Isaiah 11:9

Chapter 14
1. Numbers 22:20-35
2. Jeremiah 32:27

Chapter 15
1. Phillipians 4:7
2. Psalm 37:4
3. 1 Corinthians 13:12

Other Notes

1. Randy Alcorn (Founder of Eternal Perspective Ministries), *Heaven*, (Carol Stream, IL: Tyndale House Publishers, 2011).
2. Max Lucado, *In The Grip Of Grace*, (Nashville, TN: Thomas Nelson Publishing,1996).
3. Max Lucado, *John 3:16 The Numbers Of Hope*, (Nashville, TN: Thomas Nelson Publishing, 2007).
4. Niki Behrikis Shanahan, *Who Says Animals Go To Heaven? A Collection of 60 Prominent Christian Leaders*, (Tyngsborough, MA: *Pete Publishing*, 2008).
5. Niki Behrikis Shanahan, *There is Eternal Life For Animals*, (Tyngsborough, MA: *Pete Publishing*, 2002).
6. Todd & Sonja Burpo, *Heaven Changes Everything*, (Nashville, TN: Thomas Nelson Publishing, 2012).
7. James Daly, "Do Pets Go To Heaven?"(Colorado Springs, Colorado: *Focus on the Family*, 2010).
8. *Scott Ross Commentary*, Do All Dogs Really Go to Heaven? (Virginia Beach, VA: *700 Club*).
9. Scott Ross, "Heavenbound?: Responses to Pets in the Afterlife," (Virginia Beach, Virginia: *700 Club*,).
10. Rome Neal, "The Evolving Roles Of Dogs" with Jon Katz-The New Work Of Dogs. (CBS Online Web page: *CBS News*, 2003).
11. Hugh Ross, "Hidden Treasures in the Book of Job," (Virginia Beach, VA: *700 Club*).
12. Pat Robertson, "200 Questions," (Virginia Beach, VA: *CBN*).
13. Craig Von Buseck, "Three Parts of Man," (Virginia Beach, VA: *700 Club*).
14. Craig Von Buseck, "Noah's Ark: How Were The Animals Gathered," (Virginia Beach, VA: *700 Club*).
15. Billy Graham, "Will There Be Animals In Heaven," (Charlotte, NC: Tribune Media Services, 2013).
16. Dr. J.Rodman Williams (Theologian), "Theology Q&A,"(Virginia Beach, VA: *CBN*).
17. "Foundations of Our Faith," Operation Good Shepherd Series (Virginia Beach, VA: *CBN online series*)
18. J.R. Robison, "God Wants You To Be Happy," (Virginia Beach, VA: *CBN*).
19. J.S. Lang, "Eternal Life,"(Virginia Beach, VA: *CBN*).
20. J.D. Hollowell, Ph.D, K.,"Evolution-The Ultimate Compromise,"(Virginia Beach, VA: *CBN*).
21. Hank Hanegraaff, "Pets in Heaven?" (Charlotte, NC: *Bible Answer Man*, 2011).
22. Moira Anderson Allen, M.Ed., "Do Pets Go To Heaven?" (Online article: *Clarifying Christianity*, 2002)
23. Laura Klappenbach, "How Many Animal Species Inhabit Our Planet?" (Online article: *About.Com*).
24. T. Wolosz, "How Many Species Are There?"(Online Article: *Center for Earth & Environmental Sciences*, 1988).
25. Society For Conservation Biology, "Just How Many Species Are There, Anyway?" (Online Article: *ScienceDaily*, 2003).
26. An article by an author, professor and animal advocate...Wesley Smith, Karen Swallow Prior and Ben DeVries, "Do Pets Go To Heaven," (Carol Stream, IL: *Christianity Today*, 2012).

"ANGUS"

"Angus, you are such an affectionate little guy and showed me how loyal a friend can be. I am sure you are blessing those in heaven and keeping Sage company until we join you. I surely miss you in the deepest part of my spirit that still is so entwined with yours. We all miss you. Yet even now, I feel in some unexplainable way, that we are communicating the love we have for each other. I so look forward to all of us being together forever in our heavenly home with the Lord."

"UNTIL HEAVEN THEN MY FRIEND, WHEN I SEE YOU AGAIN."

Follow Tana on
Her Blog: www.tanaosborn.com
Facebook: tanaosborn@facebook.com
Twitter: https://twitter.com/TanaOsborn

www.ingramcontent.com/pod-product-compliance
Lightning Source LLC
Chambersburg PA
CBHW070645030426

42337CB00020B/4169